George C. Wolfe

The Colored Museum

Music by Kysia Bostic

D0972803

357 W 20th St., NY NY 10011
212 627-1055

First printing: May 1987
Second printing: January 1990
Third printing: August 1992
ISBN: 0-88145-052-9

Design by Marie Donovan.
Front cover design by Paul Davis Studio.
Set in Aster by L&F Technical Composition, Lakeland, FL.
Printed on recycled acid-free paper and bound in the USA.

ABOUT THE AUTHOR

George C. Wolfe was awarded a CBS/Foundation of the Dramatist Guild Playwrighting Award for *The Colored Museum*. He is the librettist for "Queenie Pie," Duke Ellington's opera, which had its world premiere at The American Music Theatre Festival, a subsequent production at The Kennedy Center, and is slated to appear on Broadway in Fall 1987. He has received grants from The Rockefeller Foundation, The National Endowment for the Arts, and The National Institute for Musical Theatre. Mr. Wolfe is a contributing author to *The Living Theatre,* published by McGraw-Hill. Originally from Frankfort, KY, he holds a B.A. in Directing from Pomona College and an M.F.A. in Dramatic Writing/Musical Theatre from NYU.

The Colored Museum had its world premiere at the Crossroads Theatre Company on 26 March 1986. Rick Khan was the Executive Director; Lee Richardson, the Artistic Director who directed the following cast:

> Arnold Bankston
> Olivia Virgil Harper
> Robert Jason
> Myra Taylor
> Vickilyn Reynolds
> and Natasha Durant as THE LITTLE GIRL

Brian Martin designed the set; Nancy Konrardy, the costumes; Hope Clark, the choreography; William H. Grant III, the lighting; and Rob Gorton, the sound. Kysia Bostic composed original music; Daryll Waters directed the musical and vocal arrangements. Kenneth Johnson was the Production Stage Manager. Anton Nelessen did the slide projections.

The Colored Museum previewed at Joseph Papp's New York Shakespeare Festival on 7 October 1986. It opened on 2 November 1986 with L. Kenneth Richardson directing the following cast ensemble:

> Loretta Devine
> Tommy Hollis
> Reggie Montgomery
> Vickilyn Reynolds
> Danitra Vance

Kysia Bostic was the composer/arranger; Brian Martin created the scenery, Nancy L. Konrardy, the costumes, William H. Grant III, the lighting, and Rob Gorton, the sound. Hope Clarke was the choreographer; Daryll Waters, the musical director; Anton Nelessen did the slide projections.

The Cast: An ensemble of five, two men and three women, all black, who perform all the characters that inhabit the exhibits.*

The Stage: White walls and recessed lighting. A starkness befitting a museum where the myths and madness of black/Negro/colored Americans are stored.

Built into the walls are a series of small panels, doors, revolving walls, and compartments from which actors can retrieve key props and make quick entrances.

A revolve is used, which allows for quick transitions from one exhibit to the next.

Music: All of the music for the show should be pre-recorded. Only the drummer, who is used in *Git on Board*, and then later in *Permutations* and *The Party*, is live.

THERE IS NO INTERMISSION

---

*A LITTLE GIRL, seven to twelve years old, is needed for a walk-on part in *Lala's Opening*.

The Exhibits

Git on Board
Cookin' with Aunt Ethel
The Photo Session
Soldier with a Secret
The Gospel According to Miss Roj
The Hairpiece
The Last Mama-on-the-Couch Play
Symbiosis
Lala's Opening
Permutations
The Party

The Characters

Git on Board
  MISS PAT

Cookin' with Aunt Ethel
  AUNT ETHEL

The Photo Session
  GIRL
  GUY

Soldier with a Secret
  JUNIE ROBINSON

The Gospel According to Miss Roj
  MISS ROJ
  WAITER

The Hairpiece
  THE WOMAN
  JANINE
  LAWANDA

The Last Mama-on-the-Couch Play
  NARRATOR
  MAMA
  WALTER-LEE-BEAU-WILLIE-JONES
  LADY IN PLAID
  MEDEA JONES

Symbiosis
  THE MAN
  THE KID

Lala's Opening
  LALA LAMAZING GRACE
  ADMONIA
  FLO'RANCE
  THE LITTLE GIRL

Git on Board

(*Blackness. Cut by drums pounding. Then slides, rapidly flashing before us. Images we've all seen before, of African slaves being captured, loaded onto ships, tortured. The images flash, flash, flash. The drums crescendo. Blackout. And then lights reveal* MISS PAT, *frozen. She is black, pert, and cute. She has a flip to her hair and wears a hot pink mini-skirt stewardess uniform.*)

(*She stands infront of a curtain which separates her from an offstage cockpit.*)

(*An electronic bell goes "ding" and* MISS PAT *comes to life, presenting herself in a friendly but rehearsed manner, smiling and speaking as she has done so many times before.*)

MISS PAT: Welcome aboard Celebrity Slaveship, departing the Gold Coast and making short stops at Bahia, Port Au Prince, and Havana, before our final destination of Savannah.

Hi. I'm Miss Pat and I'll be serving you here in Cabin A. We will be crossing the Atlantic at an altitude that's pretty high, so you must wear your shackles at all times.

(*She removes a shackle from the overhead compartment and demonstrates.*)

To put on your shackle, take the right hand and close the metal ring around your left hand like so. Repeat the action using your left hand to secure the right. If you have any trouble bonding yourself, I'd be more than glad to assist.

Once we reach the desired altitude, the Captain will turn off the "Fasten Your Shackle" sign ... (*She* efficiently points out the "FASTEN YOUR SHACKLE" signs on either side of her, which light up.) . . . allowing you a chance to stretch and dance in the aisles a bit. But otherwise, shackles must be worn at all times.

(*The "Fasten Your Shackles" signs go off.*)

MISS PAT: Also, we ask that you please refrain from call-and-response singing between cabins as that sort of thing can lead to rebellion. And, of course, no drums are allowed on board. Can you repeat after me, "No drums." (*She gets the audience to repeat.*) With a little more enthusiasm, please. "No drums." (*After the audience repeats it.*) That was great!

Once we're airborn, I'll be by with magazines, and earphones can be purchased for the price of your first-born male.

If there's anything I can do to make this middle passage more pleasant, press the little button over-head and I'll be with you faster than you can say, "Go down, Moses." (*She laughs at her "little joke".*) Thanks for flying Celebrity and here's hoping you have a pleasant take off.

(*The engines surge, the "Fasten Your Shackle" signs go on, and over-articulate Muzak voices are heard singing as* MISS PAT *pulls down a bucket seat and "shackles-up" for takeoff.*)

VOICES:
GET ON BOARD CELEBRITY SLAVESHIP
GET ON BOARD CELEBRITY SLAVESHIP
GET ON BOARD CELEBRITY SLAVESHIP
THERE'S ROOM FOR MANY A MORE

(*The engines reach an even, steady hum. Just as* MISS PAT *rises and replaces the shackles in the overhead compartment, the faint sound of African drumming is heard.*)

MISS PAT: Hi. Miss Pat again. I'm sorry to disturb you, but someone is playing drums. And what did we just say ... "No drums." It must be someone in Coach. But we here in Cabin A are not going to respond to those drums. As a matter of fact, we don't even hear them. Repeat after me. "I don't hear any drums." (*The audience repeats.*) And "I will not rebel."

(*The audience repeats. The drumming grows.*)

MISS PAT: (*Placating*) OK, now I realize some of us are a bit edgy after hearing about the tragedy on board The Laughing Mary, but let me assure you Celebrity has no intention of throwing you overboard and collecting the insurance. We value you!

(*She proceeds to single out individual passengers/audience members.*)

Why the songs *you* are going to sing in the cotton fields, under the burning heat and stinging lash, will metamorphose and give birth to the likes of James Brown and the Fabulous Flames. And you, yes *you*, are going to come up with some of the best dances. The best dances! The Watusi! The Funky Chicken! And just think of what *you* are going to mean to William Faulkner.

All right, so you're gonna have to suffer for a few hundred years, but from your pain will come a culture so complex. *And*, with this little item here ... (*She removes a basketball from the overhead compartment.*) ... you'll become millionares!

(*There is a roar of thunder. The lights quiver and the "Fasten Your Shackle" signs begin to flash. MISS PAT quickly replaces the basketball in the overhead compartment and speaks very reassuringly.*)

Miss Pat: No, don't panic. I'm here to take care of you. We're just flying through a little thunder storm. Now the only way you're going to make it through

this one is if you abandon your God and worship a
new one. So, on the count of three, let's all sing. One,
two, three ...

NOBODY KNOWS DE TROUBLE I SEEN

Oh, I forgot to mention, when singing, omit the T-H
sound. "The" becomes "de". "They" becomes "dey".
Got it? Good!

NOBODY KNOWS ...
NOBODY KNOWS ...

Oh, so you don't like that one? Well then let's try
another—

SUMMER TIME
AND DE LIVIN' IS EASY

Gershwin. He comes from another oppressed people
so he understands.

FISH ARE JUMPIN' ... come on.
AND DE COTTON IS HIGH.

Sing, damnit!

(*Lights begin to flash, the engines surge, and there is
wild drumming.* MISS PAT *sticks her head through the
curtain and speaks with an offstage* CAPTAIN.)

MISS PAT: What?

VOICE OF CAPTAIN (*O.S.*): Time warp!

MISS PAT: Time warp! (*She turns to the audience and
puts on a pleasant face.*) The Captain has assured me
everything is fine. We're just caught in a little time
warp. (*Trying to fight her growing hysteria.*) On your
right you will see the American Revolution, which
will give the U.S. of A exclusive rights to your life.
And on your left, the Civil War, which means you will
vote Republican until F.D.R. comes along. And now

we're passing over the Great Depression, which means everybody gets to live the way you've been living. (*There is a blinding flash of light, and an explosion. She screams.*) Ahhhhhhhhh! That was World War I, which is not to be confused with World War II ... (*There is a larger flash of light, and another explosion.*) ... Ahhhhh! Which is not to be confused with the Korean War or the Vietnam War, all of which you will play a major role in.

Oh, look, now we're passing over the sixties. Martha and Vandellas ... Malcolm X. (*There is a gun shot.*) ... "Julia" with Miss Diahann Carroll ... and five little girls in Sunday school ... (*There is an explosion.*) Martin Luther King ... (*A gun shot*) Oh no! The Supremes just broke up! (*The drumming intensifies.*) Stop playing those drums. I said, stop playing those damn drums. You can't stop history! You can't stop time! Those drums will be confiscated once we reach Savannah. Repeat after me. I don't hear any drums and I will not rebel. I will not rebel! I will not re—

(*The lights go out, she screams, and the sound of a plane landing and screeching to a halt is heard. After a beat, lights reveal a wasted, disheveled* MISS PAT, *but perky nonetheless.*)

MISS PAT: Hi. Miss Pat here. Things got a bit jumpy back there, but the Captain has just informed me we have safely landed in Savannah. Please check the overhead before exiting as any baggage you don't claim, we trash.

It's been fun, and we hope the next time you consider travel, it's with Celebrity.

(*Luggage begins to revolve onstage from offstage left, going past* MISS PAT *and revolving offstage right. Mixed in with the luggage are two male slaves and a woman slave, complete with luggage and I.D. tags around their necks.*)

MISS PAT: (*With routine, rehearsed pleasantness.*)
Have a nice day. Bye bye.
Button up that coat, it's kind of chilly.
Have a nice day. Bye bye.
You take care now.
See you.
Have a nice day.
Have a nice day.
Have a nice day.

Cookin' with Aunt Ethel

(*As the slaves begin to revolve off, a low-down gut-bucket blues is heard.* AUNT ETHEL, *a down-home black woman with a bandana on her head, revolves to center stage. She stands behind a big black pot and wears a reassuring grin.*)

AUNT ETHEL: Welcome to "Aunt Ethel's Down-Home Cookin' Show," where we explores the magic and mysteries of colored cuisine.

Today, we gonna be servin' ourselves up some . . . (*She laughs.*) I'm not gonna tell you. That's right! I'm not gonna tell you what it is till after you done cooked it. Child, on "The Aunt Ethel Show" we loves to have ourselves some fun. Well, are you ready? Here goes.

(*She belts out a hard-drivin' blues and throws invisible ingredients into the big, black pot.*)

FIRST YA ADD A PINCH OF STYLE
AND THEN A DASH OF FLAIR
NOW YA STIR IN SOME PREOCCUPATION
WITH THE TEXTURE OF YOUR HAIR

NEXT YA ADD ALL KINDS OF RHYTHMS
LOTS OF FEELINGS AND PIZZAZ
THEN HUNNY THROW IN SOME RAGE
TILL IT CONGEALS AND TURNS TO JAZZ

NOW YOU COOKIN'
COOKIN' WITH AUNT ETHEL
YOU REALLY COOKIN'
COOKIN' WITH AUNT ETHEL, OH YEAH

NOW YA ADD A HEAP OF SURVIVAL
AND HUMILITY, JUST A TOUCH
ADD SOME ATTITUDE
OPPS! I PUT TOO MUCH

AND NOW A WHOLE LOT OF HUMOR
SALTY LANGUAGE, MIXED WITH SADNESS
THEN THROW IN A BOX OF BLUES
AND SIMMER TO MADNESS

NOW YOU COOKIN'
COOKIN' WITH AUNT ETHEL, OH YEAH!

NOW YOU BEAT IT—REALLY WORK IT
DISCARD AND DISOWN
AND IN A FEW HUNDRED YEARS
ONCE IT'S AGED AND FULLY GROWN
YA PUT IT IN THE OVEN
TILL IT'S BLACK
AND HAS A SHEEN
OR TILL IT'S NICE AND YELLA
OR ANY SHADE IN BETWEEN

NEXT YA TAKE 'EM OUT AND COOL 'EM
'CAUSE THEY NO FUN WHEN THEY HOT
AND WON'T YOU BE SURPRISED
AT THE CONCOCTION YOU GOT

YOU HAVE BAKED
BAKED YOURSELF A BATCH OF NEGROES
YES YOU HAVE BAKED YOURSELF
BAKED YOURSELF A BATCH OF NEGROES

(*She pulls from the pot a handful of Negroes, black dolls.*)

But don't ask me what to do with 'em now that you got 'em, 'cause child, that's your problem (*She throws the dolls back into the pot.*) But in any case, yaw be sure to join Aunt Ethel next week, when we gonna be servin' ourselves up some chitlin quiche ... some grits-under-glass,

AND A SWEET POTATO PIE
AND YOU'LL BE COOKIN'
COOKIN' WITH AUNT ETHEL
OH YEAH!

(*On* AUNT ETHEL'S *final rift, lights reveal* ...)

The Photo Session

(*. . . a very glamorous, gorgeous, black couple, wearing the best of everything and perfect smiles. The stage is bathed in color and bright white light. Disco music with the chant: "We're fabulous" plays in the background. As they pose, larger-than-life images of their perfection are projected on the museum walls. The music quiets and the images fade away as they begin to speak and pose.*)

GIRL: The world was becoming too much for us.

GUY: We couldn't resolve the contradictions of our existence.

GIRL: And we couldn't resolve yesterday's pain.

GUY: So we gave away our life and we now live inside *Ebony Magazine.*

GIRL: Yes, we live inside a world where everyone is beautiful, and wears fabulous clothes.

GUY: And no one says anything profound.

GIRL: Or meaningful.

GUY: Or contradictory.

GIRL: Because no one talks. Everyone just smiles and shows off their cheekbones.

(*They adopt a profile pose.*)

Last month I was black and fabulous while holding up a bottle of vodka.

GIRL: This month we get to be black and fabulous together.

(*They dance/pose. The "We're fabulous" chant builds and then fades as they start to speak again.*)

GIRL: There are of course setbacks.

GUY: We have to smile like this for a whole month.

GIRL: And we have no social life.

GUY: And no sex.

GIRL: And at times it feels like we're suffocating, like we're not human anymore.

GUY: And everything is rehearsed, including this other kind of pain we're starting to feel.

GIRL: The kind of pain that comes from feeling no pain at all.

(*They then speak and pose with a sudden burst of energy.*)

GUY: But one can't have everything.

GIRL: Can one?

GUY: So if the world is becoming too much for you, do like we did.

GIRL: Give away your life and come be beautiful with us.

GUY: We guarantee, no contradictions.

GIRL/GUY: Smile/click, smile/click, smile/click.

GIRL: And no pain.

(*They adopt a final pose and revolve off as the "We're fabulous" chant plays and fades into the background.*)

A Soldier with a Secret

(*Projected onto the museum walls are the faces of black soldiers—from the Spanish-American thru to the Vietnam War. Lights slowly reveal JUNIE ROBINSON, a black combat soldier, posed on an onyx plinth. He comes to life and smiles at the audience. Somewhat dim-witted, he has an easy-going charm about him.*)

JUNIE: Pst. Pst. I know the secret. The secret to your pain. 'Course, I didn't always know. First I had to die, then come back to life, 'fore I had the gift.

Ya see the Cappin sent me off up ahead to scout for screamin' yella bastards. 'Course, for the life of me I couldn't understand why they'd be screamin', seein' as how we was tryin' to kill them and they us.

But anyway, I'm off lookin', when all of a sudden I find myself caught smack dead in the middle of this explosion. This blindin' burnin', scaldin', explosion. Musta been a booby trap or something, 'cause all around me is fire. Hell, I'm on fire. Like a piece of chicken dropped in a skillet of cracklin' grease. Why, my flesh was justa peelin' off of my bones.

But then I says to myself, "Junie, if yo' flesh is on fire, how come you don't feel no pain!" And I didn't. I swear as I'm standin' here, I felt nuthin. That's when I sort of put two and two together and realized I didn't feel no whole lot of hurtin' cause I done died.

Well I just picked myself up and walked right on out of that explosion. Hell, once you know you dead, why keep on dyin', ya know?

So, like I say, I walk right outta that explosion, fully expectin' to see white clouds, Jesus, and my Mama, only all I saw was more war. Shootin' goin' on way off in this direction and that direction. And there, standin' around, was all the guys. Hubert, J.F., the Cappin. I guess the sound of the explosion must of attracted 'em, and they all starin' at me like I'm some kind of ghost.

So I yells to 'em, "Hey there Hubert! Hey there Cappin!" But they just stare. So I tells 'em how I'd died and how I guess it wasn't my time cause here I am, "Fully in the flesh and not a scratch to my bones." And they still just stare. So I took to starin' back.

(*The expression on* JUNIE's *face slowly turns to horror and disbelief.*)

Only what I saw . . . well I can't exactly to this day describe it. But I swear, as sure as they was wearin' green and holdin' guns, they was each wearin' a piece of the future on their faces.

Yeah. All the hurt that was gonna get done to them and they was gonna do to folks was right there clear as day.

I saw how J.F., once he got back to Chicago, was gonna get shot dead by this po-lice, and I saw how Hubert was gonna start beatin' up on his old lady which I didn't understand, 'cause all he could do was talk on and on about how much he loved her. Each and every one of 'em had pain in his future and blood on his path. And God or the Devil one spoke to me and said, "Junie, these colored boys ain't gonna be the same after this war. They ain't gonn have no kind of happiness."

Well right then and there it come to me. The secret to their pain.

Late that night, after the medics done checked me over and found me fit for fightin', after everybody done settle down for the night, I sneaked over to where Hubert was sleepin', and with a needle I stole from the medics . . . pst, pst . . . I shot a little air into his veins. The second he died, all the hurtin-to-come just left his face.

Two weeks later I got J.F. and after that Woodrow . . . Jimmy Joe . . . I even spent all night waitin' by the latrine 'cause I knew the Cappin always made a late night visit and pst . . . pst . . . I got him.

(*Smiling, quite proud of himself.*) That's how come I died and come back to life. 'Cause just like Jesus went around healin' the sick, I'm supposed to go around healin' the hurtin' all these colored boys wearin' from the war.

Pst, pst. I know the secret. The secret to your pain. The secret to yours, and yours. Pst. Pst. Pst. Pst.

(*The lights slowly fade.*)

The Gospel According to Miss Roj

(*The darkness is cut by electronic music. Cold, pounding, unrelenting. A neon sign which spells out THE BOTTOMLESS PIT clicks on. There is a lone bar stool. Lights flash on and off, pulsating to the beat. There is a blast of smoke and, from the haze, MISS ROJ appears. He is dressed in striped patio pants, white go-go boots, a halter, and cat-shaped sunglasses. What would seem ridiculous on anyone else, MISS ROJ wears as if it were high fashion. He carries himself with total elegance and absolute arrogance.*)

MISS ROJ: God created black people and black people created style. The name's Miss Roj ... that's R.O.J. thank you and you can find me every Wednesday, Friday and Saturday nights at "The Bottomless Pit," the watering hole for the wild and weary which asks the question, "Is there life after Jherri-curl?"

(*A waiter enters, hands, MISS ROJ a drink, and then exits.*)

Thanks, doll. Yes, if they be black and swish, the B.P. has seen them, which is not to suggest the Pit is lacking in cultural diversity. Oh no. There are your dinge queens, white men who like their chicken legs dark. (*He winks/flirts with a man in the audience.*) And let's not forget, "Los Muchachos de la Neighborhood." But the speciality of the house is The Snap Queens. (*He snaps his fingers.*) We are a rare breed.

For, you see, when something strikes our fancy, when the truth comes piercing through the dark, well you just can't let it pass unnoticed. No darling. You must pronounce it with a snap. (*He snaps.*)

Snapping comes from another galaxy, as do all snap queens. That's right. I ain't just your regular oppressed American Negro. No-no-no! I am an extraterrestial. And I ain't talkin' none of that shit you seen in the movies! I have real power.

(*The waiter enters.* MISS ROJ *stops him.*)

Speaking of no power, will you please tell Miss Stingy-with-the-rum, that if Miss Roj had wanted to remain sober, she could have stayed home and drank Kool-aid. (*He snaps.*) Thank you.

(*The waiter exits.* MISS ROJ *crosses and sits on bar stool.*)

Yes, I was placed here on Earth to study the life habits of a deteriorating society, and child when we talkin' New York City, we are discussing the Queen of Deterioration. Miss New York is doing a slow dance with death, and I am here to warn you all, but before I do, I must know . . . don't you just love my patio pants? Annette Funicello immortalized them in "Beach Blanket Bingo," and I have continued the legacy. And my go-gos? I realize white after Labor Day is very gauche, but as the saying goes, if you've got it flaunt it, if you don't, front it and snap to death any bastard who dares to defy you. (*Laughing*) Oh ho! My demons are showing. Yes, my demons live at the bottom of my Bacardi and Coke.

Let's just hope for all concerned I dance my demons out before I drink them out 'cause child, dancing demons take you on a ride, but those drinkin' demons just take you, and you find yourself doing the strangest things. Like the time I locked my father in the broom closet. Seems the liquor made his tongue real liberal and he decided he was gonna baptize me with the word "faggot" over and over. Well, he's just going on and on with "faggot this" and "faggot that," all the while walking toward the broom closet to piss. Poor drunk bastard was just all turned around. So the demons just took hold of my wedges and forced me to kick the drunk son-of-a-bitch into the closet and lock the door. (*Laughter*) Three days later I remembered he was there. (*He snaps.*)

(*The waiter enters.* MISS ROJ *takes a drink and downs it.*)

Another!

(*The waiter exits.*)

(*Dancing about.*) Oh yes-yes-yes! Miss Roj is quintes-
sential style. I corn row the hairs on my legs so that
they spell out M.I.S.S. R.O.J. And I dare any bastard
to fuck with me because I will snap your ass into
oblivion.

I have the power, you know. Everytime I snap, I steal
one beat of your heart. So if you find yourself gasp-
ing for air in the middle of the night, chances are you
fucked with Miss Roj and she didn't like it.

Like the time this asshole at Jones Beach decided to
take issue with my coulotte-sailor ensemble. This
child, this muscle-bound Brooklyn thug in a skin-
tight bikini, very skin-tight so the whole world can
see that instead of a brain, God gave him an extra
thick piece of sausage. You know the kind who beat
up on their wives for breakfast. Well, he decided to
blurt out when I walked by, "Hey look at da monkey
coon in da faggit suit." Well, I walked up to the poor
dear, very calmly lifted my hand, and. . . . (*He snaps
in rapid succession.*) A heart attack, right there on the
beach. (*He singles out someone in the audience.*) You
don't believe it? Cross me! Come on! Come on!

(*The waiter enters, hands* MISS ROJ *a drink.* MISS ROJ
downs it. The waiter exits.)

(*Looking around.*) If this place is the answer, we're
asking all the wrong questions. The only reason I
come here is to communicate with my origins. The
flashing lights are signals from my planet way out
there. Yes, girl, even further than Flatbush. We're
talking another galaxy. The flashing lights tell me
how much time is left before the end.

(*Very drunk and loud by now.*) I hate the people here. I hate the drinks. But most of all I hate this goddamn music. That ain't music. Give me Aretha Franklin any day. (*Singing*) "Just a little respect. R.E.S.P.E.C.T." Yeah! Yeah!

Come on and dance your last dance with Miss Roj. Last call is but a drink away and each snap puts you one step closer to the end.

A high-rise goes up. You can't get no job. Come on everybody and dance. A whole race of people gets trashed and debased. Snap those fingers and dance. Some sick bitch throws her baby out the window 'cause she thinks it's the Devil. Everybody snap! *The New York Post.* Snap!

Snap for every time you walk past someone lying in the street, smelling like frozen piss and shit and you don't see it. Snap for every crazed bastard who kills himself so as to get the jump on being killed. And snap for every sick muthafucker who, bored with carrying around his fear, takes to shooting up other people.

Yeah, snap your fingers and dance with Miss Roj. But don't be fooled by the banners and balloons 'cause, child, this ain't no party going on. Hell no! It's a wake. And the casket's made out of stone, steel, and glass and the people are racing all over the pavement like maggots on a dead piece of meat.

Yeah, dance! But don't be surprised if there ain't no beat holding you together 'cause we traded in our drums for respectability. So now it's just words. Words rappin'. Words screechin'. Words flowin' instead of blood 'cause you know that don't work. Words cracklin' instead of fire 'cause by the time a match is struck on 125th Street and you run to midtown, the flame has been blown away.

So come on and dance with Miss Roj and her demons. We don't ask for acceptance. We don't ask for approval. We know who we are and we move on it!

I guarantee you will never hear two fingers put together in a snap and not think of Miss Roj. That's power, baby. Patio pants and all.

(*The lights begin to flash in rapid succession.*)

So let's dance! And snap! And dance! And snap!

(MISS ROJ *begins to dance as if driven by his demons. There is a blast of smoke and when the haze settles,* MISS ROJ *has revolved off and in place of him is a recording of Aretha Franklin singing, "Respect."*)

The Hairpiece

(*As "Respect" fades into the background, a vanity revolves to center stage. On this vanity are two wigs, an Afro wig, circa 1968, and a long, flowing wig, both resting on wig stands. A black* WOMAN *enters, her head and body wrapped in towels. She picks up a framed picture and after a few moments of hesitation, throws it into a small trash can. She then removes one of her towels to reveal a totally bald head. Looking into a mirror on the "fourth wall," she begins applying makeup.*)

(*The wig stand holding the Afro wig opens her eyes. Her name is* JANINE. *She stares in disbelief at the bald woman.*)

JANINE: (*Calling to the other wig stand.*) LaWanda. LaWanda girl, wake up.

(*The other wig stand, the one with the long, flowing wig, opens her eyes. Her name is* LAWANDA.)

LAWANDA: What? What is it?

JANINE: Check out girlfriend.

LAWANDA: Oh, girl, I don't believe it.

JANINE: (*Laughing*) Just look at the poor thing, trying to paint some life onto that face of hers. You'd think by now she'd realize it's the hair. It's all about the hair.

LAWANDA: What hair! She ain't go no hair! She done fried, dyed, de-chemicalized her shit to death.

JANINE: And all that's left is that buck-naked scalp of hers, sittin' up there apologizin' for being odd-shaped and ugly.

LAWANDA: (*Laughing with* JANINE.) Girl, stop!

JANINE: I ain't sayin' nuthin' but the truth.

LaWANDA/JANINE: The bitch is bald! (*They laugh.*)

JANINE: And all over some man.

LaWANDA: I tell ya, girl, I just don't understand it. I mean, look at her. She's got a right nice face, a good head on her shoulders. A good job even. And she's got to go fall in love with that fool.

JANINE: That political quick-change artist. Everytime the nigga went and changed his ideology, she went and changed her hair to fit the occasion.

LaWANDA: Well at least she's breaking up with him.

JANINE: Hunny, no!

LaWANDA: Yes child.

JANINE: Oh, girl, dish me the dirt!

LaWANDA: Well, you see, I heard her on the phone, talking to one of her girlfriends, and she's meeting him for lunch today to give him the ax.

JANINE: Well it's about time.

LaWANDA: I hear ya. But don't you worry 'bout a thing, girlfriend. I'm gonna tell you all about it.

JANINE: Hunny, you won't have to tell me a damn thing 'cause I'm gonna be there, front row, center.

LaWANDA: You?

JANINE: Yes, child, she's wearing me to lunch.

LaWANDA: (*Outraged*) I don't think so!

JANINE: (*With an attitude*) What do you mean, you don't think so?

LaWANDA: Exactly what I said, "I don't think so." Damn, Janine, get real. How the hell she gonna wear both of us?

JANINE: She ain't wearing both of us. She's wearing me.

LaWanda: Says who?

Janine: Says me! Says her! Ain't that right, girl-friend?

(*The* Woman *stops putting on makeup, looks around, sees no one, and goes back to her makeup.*)

Janine: I said, ain't that right!

(*The* Woman *picks up the phone.*)

Woman: Hello . . . hello . . .

Janine: Did you hear the damn phone ring?

Woman: No.

Janine: Then put the damn phone down and talk to me.

Woman: I ah . . . don't understand.

Janine: It ain't deep so don't panic. Now, you're having lunch with your boyfriend, right?

Woman: (*Breaking into tears.*) I think I'm having a nervous breakdown.

Janine: (*Impatient*) I said you're having lunch with your boyfriend, right!

Woman: (*Scared, pulling herself together.*) Yes, right . . . right.

Janine: To break up with him.

Woman: How did you know that?

LaWanda: I told her.

Woman: (*Stands and screams.*) Help! Help!

Janine: Sit down. I said sit your ass down!

(*The* Woman *does.*)

Janine: Now set her straight and tell her you're wearing me.

LaWANDA: She's the one that needs to be set straight, so go on and tell her you're wearing me.

JANINE: No, tell her you're wearing me.

(*There is a pause.*)

LaWANDA: Well?

JANINE: Well?

WOMAN: I ah . . . actually hadn't made up my mind.

JANINE: (*Going off*) What do you mean you ain't made up you mind! After all that fool has put you through, you gonna need all the attitude you can get and there is nothing like attitude and a healthy head of kinks to make his shit shrivel like it should!

That's right! When you wearin' me, you lettin' him know he ain't gonna get no sweet-talkin' comb through your love without some serious resistance. No-no! The kink of my head is like the kink of your heart and neither is about to be hot-pressed into surrender.

LaWANDA: That shit is so tired. The last time attitude worked on anybody was 1968. Janine girl, you need to get over it and get on with it. (*To the* WOMAN.) And you need to give the nigga a goodbye he will never forget.

I say give him hysteria! Give him emotion! Give him rage! And there is nothing like a toss of the tresses to make your emotional outburst shine with emotional flair.

You can toss me back, shake me from side to side, all the while screaming, "I want you out of my life forever!!!" And not only will I come bouncing back for more, but you just might win an Academy Award for best performance by a head of hair in a dramatic role.

JANINE: Miss hunny, please! She don't need no Barbie doll dipped in chocolate telling her what to do. She needs a head of hair that's coming from a fo' real place.

LaWANDA: Don't you dare talk about nobody coming from a "fo' real place," Miss Made-in-Taiwan!

JANINE: Hey! I ain't ashamed of where I come from. Besides, it don't matter where you come from as long as you end up in the right place.

LaWANDA: And it don't matter the grade as long as the point gets made. So go on and tell her you're wearing me.

JANINE: No, tell her you're wearing me.

(*The* WOMAN, *unable to take it, begins to bite off her fake nails, as* LaWANDA *and* JANINE *go at each other.*)

LaWANDA:
Set the bitch straight. Let her know there is no way she could even begin to compete with me. I am quality. She is kink. I am exotic. She is common. I am class and she is trash. That's right. T.R.A.S.H. We're talking three strikes and you're out. So go on and tell her you're wearing me. Go on, tell her! Tell her! Tell her!

JANINE:
Who you callin' a bitch? Why, if I had hands I'd knock you clear into next week. You think you cute. She thinks she's cute just 'cause that synthetic mop of hers blows in the wind. She looks like a fool and you look like an even bigger fool when you wear her, so go on and tell her you're wearing me. Go on, tell her! Tell her! Tell her!

(*The* WOMAN *screams and pulls the two wigs off the wig stands as the lights go to black on three bald heads.*)

The Last Mama-on-the-Couch Play

(*A* NARRATOR, *dressed in a black tuxedo, enters through the audience and stands center stage. He is totally solemn.*)

NARRATOR: We are pleased to bring you yet another Mama-on-the-Couch play. A searing domestic drama that tears at the very fabric of racist America. (*He crosses upstage center and sits on a stool and reads from a playscript.*) Act One. Scene One.

(MAMA *revolves on stage left, sitting on a couch reading a large, oversized Bible. A window is placed stage right.* MAMA'S *dress, the couch, and drapes are made from the same material. A doormat lays down center.*)

NARRATOR: Lights up on a dreary, depressing, but with middle-class aspirations tenement slum. There is a couch, with a Mama on it. Both are well worn. There is a picture of Jesus on the wall . . . (*A picture of Jesus is instantly revealed.*) . . . and a window which looks onto an abandoned tenement. It is late spring

Enter Walter-Lee-Beau-Willie-Jones (SON *enters through the audience.*) He is Mama's thirty-year-old son. His brow is heavy from three hundred years of oppression.

MAMA: (*Looking up from her Bible, speaking in a slow manner.*) Son, did you wipe your feet?

SON: (*An ever-erupting volcano.*) No, Mama, I didn't wipe me feet! Out there, every day, Mama is the Man. The Man Mama. Mr. Charlie! Mr. Bossman! And he's wipin' his feet on me. On me, Mama, every damn day of my life. Ain't that enough for me to deal with? Ain't that enough?

MAMA: Son, wipe your feet.

SON: I wanna dream. I wanna be somebody. I wanna take charge of my life.

MAMA: You can do all of that, but first you got to wipe your feet.

SON: (*As he crosses to the mat, mumbling and wiping his feet.*) Wipe my feet . . . wipe my feet . . . wipe my feet . . .

MAMA: That's a good boy.

SON: (*Exploding*) Boy! Boy! I don't wanna be nobody's good boy, Mama. I wanna be my own man!

MAMA: I know son, I know. God will show the way.

SON: God, Mama! Since when did your God ever do a damn thing for the black man. Huh, Mama, huh? You tell me. When did your God ever help me.

MAMA: (*Removing her wire-rim glasses.*) Son, come here.

(SON *crosses to* MAMA, *who slowly stands and in a exaggerated stage slap, backhands* SON *clear across the stage. The* NARRATOR *claps his hands to create the sound for the slap.* MAMA *then lifts her clinched fists to the heavens.*)

MAMA: Not in my house, my house, will you ever talk that way again!

(*The* NARRATOR, *so moved by her performance, erupts in applause and encourages the audience to do so.*)

NARRATOR: Beautiful. Just stunning.

(*He reaches into one of the secret compartments of the set and gets an award which he ceremoniously gives to* MAMA *for her performance. She bows and then returns to the couch.*)

NARRATOR: Enter Walter-Lee-Beau-Willie's wife, The Lady in Plaid.

(*Music from nowhere is heard, a jazzy pseudo-abstract intro as the* LADY IN PLAID *dances in through the audience, wipes her feet, and then twirls about.*)

LADY:
She was a creature of regal beauty
who in ancient time graced the temples of the Nile
with her womanliness
But here she was, stuck being colored
and a woman in a world that valued neither.

SON: You cooked my dinner?

LADY: (*Oblivious to* SON.)
Feet flat, back broke,
she looked at the man who, though he be thirty,
still ain't got his own apartment.
Yeah, he's still livin' with his Mama!
And she asked herself, was this the life
for a Princess Colored, who by the
translucence of her skin, knew the
universe was her sister.

(*The* LADY IN PLAID *twirls and dances.*)

SON: (*Becoming irate.*) I've had a hard day of dealin'
with the Man. Where's my damn dinner? Woman,
stand still when I'm talkin' to you!

LADY: And she cried for her sisters in Detroit
Who knew, as she, that their souls belonged
in ancient temples on the Nile.
And she cried for her sisters in Chicago
who, like her, their life has become
one colored hell.

SON: There's only one thing gonna get through to you.

LADY: And she cried for her sisters in New Orleans
And her sisters in Trenton and Birmingham,
and
Poughkeepsie and Orlando and Miami Beach
and
Las Vegas, Palm Springs.

(*As she continues to call out cities, he crosses offstage and returns with two black dolls and then crosses to the window.*)

SON: Now are you gonna cook me dinner?

LADY: Walter-Lee-Beau-Willie-Jones, No! Not my babies.

(SON *throws them out the window. The* LADY IN PLAID *then lets out a primal scream.*)

LADY: He dropped them!!!!

(*The* NARRATOR *breaks into applause.*)

NARRATOR: Just splendid. Shattering.

(*He thens crosses and after an intense struggle with* MAMA, *he takes the award from her and gives it to the* LADY IN PLAID, *who is still suffering primal pain.*)

LADY: Not my babies ... not my ... (*Upon recieving the award, she instantly recovers.*) Help me up, sugar. (*She then bows and crosses and stands behind the couch.*)

NARRATOR: Enter Medea Jones, Walter-Lee-Beau-Willie's sister.

(MEDEA *moves very ceremoniously, wiping her feet and then speaking and gesturing as if she just escaped from a Greek tragedy.*)

MEDEA:
Ah, see how the sun kneels to speak
her evening vespers, exaulting all
in her vision, even lowly tenement
long abandoned.

Mother, wife of brother, I trust
the approaching darkness finds you
safe in Hestia's busom.

Brother, why wear the face of a man
in anguish. Can the garment of thine

feelings cause the shape of your
countenance to disfigure so?

SON: (*At the end of his rope.*) Leave me alone, Medea.

MEDEA: (*To* MAMA)
Is good brother still going on and on and on
about He and The Man.

MAMA/LADY: What else?

MEDEA: Ah brother, if with our thoughts and
words we could cast thine oppressors
into the lowest bowels of wretched
hell, would that make us more like the
gods or more like our oppressors.

No, brother, no, do not let thy rage
choke the blood which anoints thy
heart with love. Forgo thine darkened
humor and let love shine on your
soul, like a jewel on a young maiden's hand.

(*Dropping to her knees.*)

I beseech thee, forgo thine
anger and leave wrath to the gods!

SON: Girl, what has gotten into you.

MEDEA: Juliard, good brother. For I am no
longer bound by rhythms of race or
region. Oh, no. My speech, like my
pain and suffering, have become
classical and therefore universal.

LADY: I didn't understand a damn thing she said, but
girl you usin' them words.

(LADY IN PLAID *crosses and gives* MEDEA *the award and
everyone applauds.*)

SON: (*Trying to stop the applause.*) Wait one damn
minute! This my play. It's about me and the Man. It
ain't got nuthin' to do with no ancient temples on the
Nile and it ain't got nuthin' to do with Hestia's

busom. And it ain't got nuthin' to do with you slap-
pin' me across no room. (*His gut-wrenching best.*) It's
about me. Me and my pain! My pain!

THE VOICE OF THE MAN: Walter-Lee-Beau-Willie, this
is the Man. You have been convicted of overacting.
Come out with your hands up.

(SON *starts to cross to the window.*)

SON: Well now that does it.

MAMA: Son, no, don't go near that window. Son, no!

(*Gun shots ring out and* SON *falls dead.*)

MAMA: (*Crossing to the body, too emotional for
words.*) My son, he was a good boy. Confused. Angry.
Just like his father. And his father's father. And his
father's father's father. And now he's dead.

(*Seeing she's about to drop to her knees, the* NAR-
RATOR *rushes and places a pillow underneath her just
in time.*)

If only he had been born into a world better than
this. A world where there are no well-worn couches
and no well-worn Mamas and nobody over emotes.

If only he had been born into an all-black musical.

(*A song intro begins.*)

Nobody ever dies in an all-black musical.

(MEDEA *and* LADY IN PLAID *pull out church fans and
begin to fan themselves.*)

MAMA: (*Singing a soul-stirring gospel.*)
OH WHY COULDN'T HE
BE BORN
INTO A SHOW WITH LOTS OF SINGING
AND DANCING

I SAY WHY
COULDN'T HE
BE BORN

LADY: Go ahead hunny. Take your time.

MAMA:
INTO A SHOW WHERE EVERYBODY
IS HAPPY

NARRATOR/MEDEA: Preach! Preach!

MAMA:
OH WHY COULDN't HE BE BORN WITH THE
    CHANCE
TO SMILE A LOT AND SING AND DANCE
OH WHY
OH WHY

OH WHY
COULDN'T HE
BE BORN
INTO AN ALL-BLACK SHOW
WOAH-WOAH

(*The* CAST *joins in, singing do-wop gospel background to* MAMA'S *lament.*)

OH WHY
COULDN'T HE
BE BORN
(HE BE BORN)
INTO A SHOW WHERE EVERBODY
IS HAPPY

WHY COULDN'T HE BE BORN WITH THE
    CHANCE
TO SMILE A LOT AND SING AND DANCE
WANNA KNOW WHY
WANNA KNOW WHY

OH WHY
COULDN'T HE
BE BORN
INTO AN ALL-BLACK SHOW
A-MEN

(*A singing/dancing, spirit-raising revival begins.*)

OH, SON, GET UP
GET UP AND DANCE
WE SAY GET UP
THIS IS YOUR SECOND CHANCE

DON'T SHAKE A FIST
JUST SHAKE A LEG
AND DO THE TWIST
DON'T SCREAM AND BEG
SON SON SON
GET UP AND DANCE

GET
GET UP
GET UP AND
GET UP AND DANCE — ALL RIGHT!
GET UP AND DANCE — ALL RIGHT!
GET UP AND DANCE!

(WALTER-LEE-BEAU-WILLIE *springs to life and joins in the dancing. A foot-stomping, hand-clapping production number takes off, which encompasses a myriad of black-Broadwayesque dancing styles—shifting speeds and styles with exuberant abandonment.*)

MAMA: (*Bluesy*)
WHY COULDN'T HE BE BORN INTO AN ALL-
  BLACK SHOW

CAST:
WITH SINGING AND DANCING

MAMA: BLACK SHOW

(MAMA *scats and the dancing becomes manic and just a little too desperate too please.*)

CAST:
WE GOTTA DANCE
WE GOTTA DANCE
GET UP GET UP GET UP AND DANCE
WE GOTTA DANCE
WE GOTTA DANCE
GOTTA DANCE!

(Just at the point the dancing is about to become violent, the cast freezes and pointedly, simply sings:)

IF WE WANT TO LIVE
WE HAVE GOT TO
WE HAVE GOT TO
DANCE ... AND DANCE ... AND DANCE ...

(As they continue to dance with zombie-like frozen smiles and faces, around them images of coon performers flash as the lights slowly fade.)

Symbiosis

(*The Temptations singing "My Girl" are heard as lights reveal a* BLACK MAN *in corporate dress standing before a large trash can throwing objects from a Saks Fifth Avenue bag into it. Circling around him with his every emotion on his face is* THE KID, *who is dressed in a late-sixties street style. His moves are slightly heightened. As the scene begins the music fades.*)

MAN: (*With contained emotions.*)
My first pair of Converse All-stars. Gone.
My first Afro-comb. Gone.
My first dashiki. Gone.
My autographed pictures of Stokley Carmichael,
    Jomo Kenyatta and Donna Summer. Gone.

KID: (*Near tears, totally upset.*) This shit's not fair man.
Damn! Hell! Shit! Shit! It's not fair!

MAN:
My first jar of Murray's Pomade.
My first can of Afro-sheen.
My first box of curl relaxer. Gone! Gone! Gone!
Eldridge Cleaver's *Soul on Ice.*

KID: Not *Soul on Ice!*

MAN: It's been replaced on my bookshelf by *The Color Purple.*

KID: (*Horrified*) No!

MAN: Gone!

KID: But—

MAN:
Jimi Hendrix's "Purple Haze." Gone.
Sly Stone's "There's A Riot Goin' On." Gone.
The Jackson Five's "I Want You Back."

KID: Man, you can't throw that away. It's living proof Michael had a black nose.

MAN: It's all going. Anything and everything that connects me to you, to who I was, to what we were, is out of my life.

KID: You've got to give me another chance.

MAN: *Fingertips Part 2.*

KID: Man, how can you do that? That's vintage Stevie Wonder.

MAN: You want to know how, Kid? You want to know how? Because my survival depends on it. Whether you know it or not, the Ice Age is upon us.

KID: (*Jokingly*) Man, what the hell you talkin' about. It's 95 damn degrees.

MAN: The climate is changing, Kid, and either you adjust or you end up extinct. A sociological dinosaur. Do you understand what I'm trying to tell you? King Kong would have made it to the top if only he had taken the elevator. Instead he brought attention to his struggle and ended up dead.

KID: (*Pleading*) I'll change. I swear I'll change. I'll maintain a low profile. You won't even know I'm around.

MAN: If I'm to become what I'm to become then you've got to go. . . . I have no history. I have no past.

KID: Just like that?

MAN: (*Throwing away a series of buttons.*) Free Angela! Free Bobby! Free Huey, Duey, and Louie! U.S. out of Viet Nam. U.S. out of Cambodia. U.S. out of Harlem, Detroit, and Newark. Gone! . . . The Temptations Greatest Hits!

KID: (*Grabbing the album.*) No!!!

MAN: Give it back, Kid.

KID: No.

MAN: I said give it back!

KID: No. I can't let you trash this. Johnny man, it contains fourteen classic cuts by the tempting Temptations. We're talking, "Ain't Too Proud to Beg," "Papa was a Rolling Stone," "My Girl."

MAN: (*Warning*) I don't have all day.

KID: For God's sake, Johnny man, "My Girl" is the jam to end all jams. It's what we are. Who we are. It's a way of life. Come on, man, for old times sake. (*Singing*)

I GOT SUNSHINE ON A CLOUDY DAY
DUM-DA-DUM-DA-DUM-DA-DUM
AND WHEN IT'S COLD OUTSIDE

Come on, Johnny man, sing

I GOT THE MONTH OF MAY

Here comes your favorite part. Come on, Johnny man, sing.

I GUESS YOU SAY
WHAT CAN MAKE ME FEEL THIS WAY
MY GIRL, MY GIRL, MY GIRL
TALKIN' 'BOUT

MAN: (*Exploding*) I said give it back!

KID: (*Angry*) I ain't givin' you a muthafuckin' thing!

MAN: Now you listen to me!

KID: No, you listen to me. This is the kid you're dealin' with, so don't fuck with me!

(*He hits his fist into his hand, and* THE MAN *grabs for his heart.* THE KID *repeats with two more hits, which causes the man to drop to the ground, grabbing his heart.*)

KID: Jai! Jai! Jai!

MAN: Kid, please.

KID: Yeah. Yeah. Now who's begging who. . . . Well, well, well, look at Mr. Cream-of-the-Crop, Mr. Colored-Man-on-Top. Now that he's making it, he no longer wants anything to do with the Kid. Well, you may put all kinds of silk ties 'round your neck and white lines up your nose, but the Kid is here to stay. You may change your women as often as you change your underwear, but the Kid is here to stay. And regardless of how much of your past that you trash, I ain't goin' no damn where. Is that clear? Is that clear?

MAN: (*Regaining his strength, beginning to stand.*) Yeah.

KID: Good. (*After a beat.*) You all right man? You all right? I don't want to hurt you, but when you start all that talk about getting rid of me, well, it gets me kind of crazy. We need each other. We are one . . .

(*Before* THE KID *can complete his sentence,* THE MAN *grabs him around his neck and starts to choke him violently.*)

MAN: (*As he strangles him.*) The . . . Ice . . . Age . . . is . . . upon us . . . and either we adjust . . . or we end up . . . extinct.

(THE KID *hangs limp in* THE MAN'S *arms.*)

MAN: (*Laughing*) Man kills his own rage. Film at eleven. (*He then dumps* THE KID *into the trash can, and closes the lid. He speaks in a contained voice.*) I have no history. I have no past. I can't. It's too much. It's much too much. I must be able to smile on cue. And watch the news with an impersonal eye. I have no stake in the madness.

Being black is too emotionally taxing; therefore I will be black only on weekends and holidays.

(*He then turns to go, but sees the Temptations album lying on the ground. He picks it up and sings quietly to himself.*)

I GUESS YOU SAY
WHAT CAN MAKE ME FEEL THIS WAY

(He pauses, but then crosses to the trash can, lifts the lid, and just as he is about to toss the album in, a hand reaches from inside the can and grabs hold of THE MAN'S *arm.* THE KID *then emerges from the can with a death grip on* THE MAN'S *arm.)*

KID: *(Smiling)* What's happenin'?

BLACKOUT

Lala's Opening

(Roving follow spots. A timpani drum roll. As we hear the voice of the ANNOUNCER, *outrageously glamorous images of* LALA *are projected onto the museum walls.)*

VOICE OF ANNOUNCER: From Rome to Rangoon! Paris to Prague! We are pleased to present the American debut of the one! The only! The breathtaking! The astounding! The stupendous! The incredible! The magnificient! Lala Lamazing Grace!

(Thunderous applause as LALA *struts on, the definitive black diva. She has long, flowing hair, an outrageous lamé dress, and an affected French accent which she loses when she's upset.)*

LALA:
EVERYBODY LOVES LALA
EVERYBODY LOVES ME
PARIS! BELIN! LONDON! ROME!
NO MATTER WHERE I GO
I ALWAYS FEEL AT HOME

OHHHH
EVERYBODY LOVES LALA
EVERYBODY LOVES ME
I'M TRES MAGNIFIQUE
AND OH SO UNIQUE
AND WHEN IT COMES TO GLAMOUR
I'M CHIC-ER THAN CHIC

(She giggles.)

THAT'S WHY EVERYBODY
EVERYBODY
EVERYBODY-EVERYBODY-EVERYBODY
LOVES ME

(She begins to vocally reach for higher and higher notes, until she has to point to her final note. She ends

the number with a grand flourish and bows to thunderous applause.)

LALA: I-love-it-I-love-it-I-love-it!

Yes, it's me! Lala Lamazing Grace and I have come home. Home to the home I never knew as home. Home to you, my people, my blood, my guts.

My story is a simple one, full of fire, passion, magique. You may ask how did I, a humble girl from the backwoods of Mississippi, come to be the ninth wonder of the modern world. Well, I can't take all of the credit. Part of it goes to him. (*She points toward the heavens.*)

No, not the light man, darling, but God. For, you see, Lala is a star. A very big star. Let us not mince words, I'm a fucking meteorite. (*She laughs.*) But He is the universe and just like my sister, Aretha la Franklin, Lala's roots are in the black church. (*She sings in a showy gospel style:*)

THAT'S WHY EVERYBODY LOVES
SWING LOW SWEET CHARIOT
THAT'S WHY EVERYBODY LOVES
GO DOWN MOSES WAY DOWN IN EGYPT LAND
THAT'S WHY EVERYBODY EVERYBODY LOVES
ME!!!

(*Once again she points to her final note and then basks in applause.*)

Thank you. Thank you.

Now, before I dazzle you with more of my limitless talent, tell me something, America. (*Musical underscoring*) Why has it taken you so long to recognize my artistry? Mother France opened her loving arms and Lala came running. All over the world Lala was embraced. But here, ha! You spat at Lala. Was I too exotic? Too much woman, or what?

Diana Ross you embrace. A too-bit nobody from Detroit, of all places. Now, I'm not knocking la Ross.

She does the best she can with the little she has. (*She laughs.*) But the Paul la Robesons, the James la Baldwins, the Josephine la Baker's, who was my godmother you know. The Lala Lamazing Grace's you kick out. You drive . . .

AWAY
I AM GOING AWAY
HOPING TO FIND A BETTER DAY
WHAT DO YOU SAY
HEY HEY
I AM GOING AWAY
AWAY

(LALA, *caught up in the drama of the song, doesn't see* ADMONIA, *her maid, stick her head out from offstage.*)

(*Once she is sure* LALA *isn't looking, she wheels onto stage right* FLO'RANCE, LALA'S *lover, who wears a white mask/blonde hair. He is gagged and tied to a chair.* ADMONIA *places him on stage and then quickly exits.*)

LALA:
AU REVOIR—JE VAIS PARTIER MAINTENANT
JE VEUX DIRE MAINTENANT
AU REVOIR
AU REVOIR
AU REVOIR
AU REVOIR
A-MA-VIE

(*On her last note, she see* FLO'RANCE *and, in total shock, crosses to him.*)

LALA: Flo'rance, what the hell are you doing out here. looking like that. I haven't seen you for three days and you decide to show up now?

(*He mumbles.*)

I don't want to hear it!

(*He mumbles.*)

I said shut up!

(ADMONIA *enters from stage right and has a letter opener on a silver tray.*)

ADMONIA: Pst!

(LALA, *embarrassed by the presence of* ADMONIA *on stage, smiles apologetically at the audience.*)

LALA: Un momento.

(*She then pulls* ADMONIA *to the side.*)

LALA: Darling, have you lost your mind coming on-stage while I'm performing. And what have you done to Flo'rance? When I asked you to keep him tied up, I didn't mean to tie him up.

(ADMONIA *gives her the letter opener.*)

LALA: Why are you giving me this? I have no letters to open. I'm in the middle of my American debut. Admonia, take Flo'rance off this stage with you! Admonia!

(ADMONIA *is gone.* LALA *turns to the audience and tries to make the best of it.*)

LALA: That was Admonia, my slightly overweight black maid, and this if Flo'rance, my amour. I remember how we met, don't you Flo'rance. I was sitting in a café on the Left Bank, when I looked up and saw the most beautiful man staring down at me.

"Who are you," he asked. I told him my name . . . whatever my name was back then. Yes, I told him my name and he said, "No, that cannot be your name. Your name should dance the way your eyes dance and your lips dance. Your name should fly, like Lala." And the rest is la history.

Flo'rance molded me into the woman I am today. He is my Svengali, my reality, my all. And I thought I was all to him, until we came here to America, and he fucked that bitch. Yeah, you fucked 'em all. Anything black and breathing. And all this time, I thought you loved me for being me. (*She holds the letter opener to his neck.*)

Well, you may think you made me, but I'll have you know I was who I was, whoever that was, long before you made me what I am. So there! (*She stabs him and breaks into song.*)

OH, LOVE CAN DRIVE A WOMAN TO MADNESS
TO PAIN AND SADNESS
I KNOW
BELIEVE ME I KNOW
I KNOW
I KNOW

(LALA *sees what she's done and is about to scream but catches herself and tries to play it off.*)

LALA: Moving right along.

(ADMONIA *enters with a telegram on a tray.*)

ADMONIA: Pst.

LALA: (*Anxious/hostile*) What is it now?

(ADMONIA *hands* LALA *a telegram.*)

LALA: (*Excited*) Oh, la telegram from one of my fans and the concert isn't even over yet. Get me the letter opener. It's in Flo'rance.

(ADMONIA *hands* LALA *the letter opener.*)

LALA: Next I am going to do for you my immortal hit song, "The Girl Inside." But first we open the telegram. (*She quickly reads it and is outraged.*) What! Which pig in la audience wrote this trash? (*Reading*) "Dear Sadie, I'm so proud. The show's wonderful, but talk less and sing more. Love, Mama."

First off, no one calls me Sadie. Sadie died the day Lala was born. And secondly, my Mama's dead.

Anyone who knows anything about Lala Lamazing
Grace knows that my mother and Josephine Baker
were French patriots together. They infiltrated a car-
nival rumored to be the center of Nazi intelligence,
disguised as Hottentot Siamese twins. You may
laugh but it's true. Mama died a heroine. It's all in
my autobiography, "Voilá Lala!" So whoever sent
this telegram is a liar!

(ADMONIA *promptly presents her with another telegram.*)

LALA: No doubt an apology. (*Reading*) "Dear Sadie,
I'm not dead. P.S. Your child misses you." What?
(*She squares off at the audience.*) Well, now, that does
it! If you are my mother, which you are not. And this
alleged child is my child, then that would mean I am
a mother and I have never given birth. I don't know
nothin' 'bout birthin' no babies! (*She laughs.*) Lala
made a funny.

So whoever sent this, show me the child! Show me!

(ADMONIA *offers another telegram.*)

LALA: (*To* ADMONIA) You know you're gonna get fired!
(*She reluctantly opens it.*) "The child is in the closet."
What closet?

ADMONIA: Pst.

(ADMONIA *pushes a button and the center wall unit
revolves around to reveal a large black door.* ADMONIA
exits, taking FLO'RANCE *with her, leaving* LALA *alone.*)

LALA: (*Laughing*) I get it. It's a plot, isn't it. A nasty little CIA, FBI kind of plot. Well let me tell you mutha-
fuckers one thing, there is nothing in that closet, real
or manufactured, that will be a dimmer to the glim-
mer of Lamé the star. You may have gotten Billie and
Bessie and a little piece of everyone else who's come
along since, but you won't get Lala. My clothes are
too fabulous! My hair is too long! My accent too
french. That's why I came home to America. To pro-
ve you ain't got nothing on me!

(*The music for her next song starts, but* LALA *is caught up in her tirade, and talks/screams over the music.*)

My mother and Josephine Baker were French patriots together! I've had brunch with the Pope! I've dined with the Queen! Everywhere I go I cause riots! Hunny, I am a star! I have transcended pain! So there! (*Yelling*) Stop the music! Stop that goddamn music.

(*The music stops.* LALA *slowly walks downstage and singles out someone in the audience.*)

Darling, you're not looking at me. You're staring at that damn door. Did you pay to stare at some fucking door or be mesmerized by my talent?

(*To the whole audience:*)

Very well! I guess I am going to have to go to the closet door, fling it open, in order to dispel all the nasty little thoughts these nasty little telegrams have planted in your nasty little minds. (*Speaking directly to someone in the audience.*) Do you want me to open the closet door? Speak up, darling, this is live. (*Once she gets the person to say "yes."*) I will open the door, but before I do, let me tell you bastards one last thing. To hell with coming home and to hell with lies and insinuations!

(LALA *goes into the closet and after a short pause comes running out, ready to scream, and slams the door. Traumatized to the point of no return, she tells the following story as if it were a jazz solo of rushing, shifting emotions.*)

LALA: I must tell you this dream I had last night. Simply magnifique. In this dream, I'm running naked in Sammy Davis Junior's hair. (*Crazed laughter*)

Yes! I'm caught in this larger than life, deep, dark forest of savage, nappy-nappy hair. The kinky-kinks are choking me, wrapped around my naked arms,

thighs, breast, face. I can't breath. And there was
nothing in that closet!

And I'm thinking if only I has a machete, I could cut
away the kinks. Remove once and for all the rough-
ness. But then I look up and it's coming toward me.
Flowing like lava. It's pomade! Ohhh, Sammy!

Yes, cakes and cakes of pomade. Making everything
nice and white and smooth and shiny, like my black/
white/black/white/black behiney.

Mama no!

And then spikes start cutting through the pomade.
Combing the coated kink. Cutting through the kink,
into me. There are bloodlines on my back. On my
thighs.

It's all over. All over . . . all over me. All over for me.

(LALA *accidentially pulls off her wig to reveal her real
hair. Stripped of her "disguise" she recoils like a
scared little girl and sings.*)

MOMMY AND DADDY
MEET AND MATE
THE CHILD THAT'S BORN
IS TORN WITH LOVE AND WITH HATE
SHE RUNS AWAY TO FIND HER OWN
AND TRIES TO DENY
WHAT SHE'S ALWAYS KNOWN
THE GIRL INSIDE

(*The closet door opens.* LALA *runs away, and a* LITTLE
BLACK GIRL *emerges from the closet. Standing behind
her is* ADMONIA.)

(*The* LITTLE GIRL *and* LALA *are in two isolated pools of
light, and mirror each other's moves until* LALA
reaches past her reflection and the LITTLE GIRL *comes
to* LALA *and they hug.* ADMONIA *then joins them as*
LALA *sings. Music underscored.*)

LALA:
WHAT'S LEFT IS THE GIRL INSIDE
THE GIRL WHO DIED
SO A NEW GIRL COULD BE BORN

SLOW FADE TO BLACK

Permutations

(*Lights up on* NORMAL JEAN REYNOLDS. *She is very Southern/country and very young. She wears a simple faded print dress and her hair, slightly mussed, is in plaits. She sits, her dress covering a large oval object.*)

NORMAL: My mama used to say, God made the exceptional, then God made the special and when God got bored, he made me. 'Course she don't say too much of nuthin' no more, not since I lay me this egg.

(*She lifts her dress to uncover a large, white egg laying between her legs.*)

Ya see it all got started when I had me sexual relations with the garbage man. Ooowee, did he smell.

No, not bad. No! He smelled of all the good things folks never shoulda thrown away. His sweat was like cantaloupe juice. His neck was like a ripe-red strawberry. And the water that fell from his eyes was like a deep, dark, juicy-juicy grape. I tell ya, it was like fuckin' a fruit salad, only I didn't spit out the seeds. I kept them here, deep inside. And three days later, my belly commence to swell, real big like.

Well my mama locked me off in some dark room, refusin' to let me see light of day 'cause, "What would the neighbors think." At first I cried a lot, but then I grew used to livin' my days in the dark, and my nights in the dark. . . . (*She hums.*) And then it wasn't but a week or so later, my mama off at church, that I got this hurtin' feelin' down here. Worse than anything I'd ever known. And then I started bleedin', real bad. I mean there was blood everywhere. And the pain had me howlin' like a near-dead dog. I tell ya, I was yellin' so loud, I couldn't even hear myself. Noooooooo! Noooooo! Carrying on something like that.

And I guess it was just too much for the body to take,
'cause the next thing I remember . . . is me coming to
and there's this big white egg layin' 'tween my legs.
First I thought somebody musta put it there as some
kind of joke. But then I noticed that all 'round this
egg were thin lines of blood that I could trace to back
between my legs.

(*Laughing*) Well, when my mama come home from
church she just about died. "Normal Jean, what's
that thing 'tween your legs? Normal Jean, you
answer me, girl!" It's not a thing, Mama. It's an egg.
And I laid it.

She tried separatin' me from it, but I wasn't havin' it.
I stayed in that dark room, huggin', holdin' onto it.

And then I heard it. It wasn't anything that coulda
been heard 'round the world, or even in the next
room. It was kinda like layin' back in the bath tub, ya
know, the water just coverin' your ears . . . and if you
lay real still and listen real close, you can hear the
sound of your heart movin' the water. You ever done
that? Well that's what it sounded like. A heart movin'
water. And it was happenin' inside here.

Why, I'm the only person I know who ever lay themselves an egg before so that makes me special. You
hear that, Mama? I'm special and so's my egg! And
special things supposed to be treated like they matter.
That's why everynight I count to it, so it knows nuthin'
never really ends. And I sing it every song I know so
that when it comes out, it's full of all kinds of feelings.
And I tell it secrets and laugh with it and . . .

(*She suddenly stops and puts her ear to the egg and
listens intently.*)

Oh! I don't believe it! I thought I heard . . . yes! (*Excited*)
Can you hear it? Instead of one heart, there's two. Two
little hearts just pattering away. Boom-boom-boom.
Boom-boom-boom. Talkin to each other like old
friends. Racin' toward the beginnin' of their lives.

(*Listening*) Oh, no, now there's three . . . four . . . five, six. More hearts than I can count. And they're all alive, beatin' out life inside my egg.

(*We begin to hear the heartbeats, drums, alive inside* NORMAL'S *egg.*)

Any day now, this egg is gonna crack open and what's gonna come out a be the likes of which nobody has ever seen. My babies! And their skin is gonna turn all kinds of shades in the sun and their hair a be growin' every which-a-way. And it won't matter and they won't care 'cause they know they are so rare and so special 'cause it's not everyday a bunch of babies break outta a white egg and start to live.

And nobody better not try and hurt my babies 'cause if they do, they gonna have to deal with me.

Yes, any day now, this shell's gonna crack and my babies are gonna fly. Fly! Fly!

(*She laughs at the thought, but then stops and says the word as if it's the most natural thing in the world.*)

Fly.

BLACKOUT

The Party

(*Before we know what's hit us, a hurricane of energy comes bounding into the space. It is* Topsy Washington. *Her hair and dress are a series of stylistic contradictions which are hip, black, and unencumbered.*)

(*Music, spiritual and funky, underscores.*)

Topsy: (*Dancing about.*) Yoho! Party! Party! Turn up the music! Turn up the music!

Have yaw ever been to a party where there was one fool in the middle of the room, dancing harder and yelling louder than everybody in the entire place. Well, hunny, that fool was me!

Yes, child! The name is Topsy Washington and I love to party. As a matter of fact, when God created the world, on the seventh day, he didn't rest. No child, he partied. Yo-ho! Party! Yeah! Yeah!

But now let me tell you 'bout this function I went to the other night, way uptown. And baby when I say way uptown, I mean way-way-way-way-way-way-way-way uptown. Somewhere's between 125th Street and infinity.

Inside was the largest gathering of black/Negro/colored Americans you'd ever want to see. Over in one corner you got Nat Turner sippin' champagne out of Eartha Kitt's slipper. And over in another corner, Bert Williams and Malcom X was discussing existentialism as it relates to the shuffle-ball-change. Girl, Aunt Jemima and Angela Davis was in the kitchen sharing a plate of greens and just goin' off about South Africa.

And then Fats sat down and started to work them eighty-eights. And then Stevie joined in. And then

Miles and Duke and Ella and Jimi and Charlie and Sly and Lightin' and Count and Louie!

And then everybody joined in. I tell you all the children was just all up in there, dancing to the rhythm of one beat. Dancing to the rhythm of their own deffinition. Celebrating in their cultural madness.

And then the floor started to shake. And the walls started to move. And before anybody knew what was happening, the entire room lifted up off the ground. The whole place just took off and went flying through space—defying logic and limitations. Just a spinning and a spinning and a spinning until it disappeared inside of my head.

(Topsy *stops dancing and regains her balance and begins to listen to the music in her head. Slowly we begin to hear it, too.*)

That's right, girl, there's a party goin' on inside of here. That's why when I walk down the street my hips just sashay all over the place. 'Cause I'm dancing to the music of the madness in me.

And whereas I used to jump into a rage anytime anybody tried to deny who I was, now all I got to do is give attitude, quicker than light, and then go on about the business of being me. 'Cause I'm dancing to the music of the madness in me.

(*As* Topsy *continues to speak,* Miss Roj, Lala, Miss Pat, *and* The Man *from SYMBIOSIS revolve on, frozen like soft sculptures.*)

Topsy: And here, all this time I been thinking we gave up our drums. But, naw, we still got 'em. I know I got mine. They're here, in my speech, my walk, my hair, my God, my style, my smile, and my eyes. And everything I need to get over in this world, is inside here, connecting me to everybody and everything that's ever been.

So, hunny, don't waste your time trying to label or define me.

(The sculptures slowly begin to come to "life" and they mirror/echo TOPSY'S *words.)*

TOPSY/EVERYBODY: . . . 'cause I'm not what I was ten years ago or ten minutes ago. I'm all of that and then some. And whereas I can't live inside yesterday's pain, I can't live without it.

(All of a sudden, madness erupts on the stage. The sculptures begin to speak all at once. Images of black/ Negro/colored Americans begin to flash—images of them dancing past the madness, caught up in the madness, being lynched, rioting, partying, surviving. Mixed in with these images are all the characters from the exhibits. Through all of this TOPSY *sings. It is a vocal and visual cacaphony which builds and builds.)*

LALA:

I must tell you about this dream I had last night. Simply magnifique. In this dream I'm running naked in Sammy Davis Junior's hair. Yes. I'm caught in this larger-than-life, deep, dark tangled forest of savage, nappy-nappy hair. Yes, the kinky kinks are choking me, are wrapped around my naked arms, my naked thighs, breast, and face, and I can't breath and there was nothing in that closet.

THE MAN:

I have no history. I have no past. I can't. It's too much. It's much too much. I must be able to smile on cue and watch the news with an impersonal eye. I have no stake in the madness.

MISS ROJ:

Snap for every time you walk past someone lying in the street smelling like frozen piss and shit and you don't see it. Snap for every crazed bastard who kills himself so as to get the jump on being killed. And snap for every sick mutha-fucker who, bored with carrying about his fear, takes to shooting up other people.

MISS PAT:

Stop playing those drums. I said stop playing those damn drums. You can't stop history. You can't stop time. Those drums will be confiscated once we reach Savannah, so give

Being black is too emotionally taxing, therefore I will be black only on weekends and holidays. them up now. Repeat after me: I don't hear any drums and I will not rebel. I will not rebel

TOPSY: (*Singing*)
THERE'S MADNESS IN ME
AND THAT MADNESS SETS ME FREE
THERE'S MADNESS IN ME
AND THAT MADNESS SETS ME FREE
THERE'S MADNESS IN ME
AND THAT MADNESS SETS ME FREE
THERE'S MADNESS IN ME
AND THAT MADNESS SETS ME FREE
THERE'S MADNESS IN ME
AND THAT MADNESS SETS ME FREE

TOPSY: My power is in my . . .

EVERYBODY: *Madness!*

TOPSY: And my colored contradictions.

(*The sculptures freeze with a smile on their faces as we hear the voice of* MISS PAT.)

VOICE OF MISS PAT: Before exiting, check the overhead as any baggage you don't claim, we trash.

BLACKOUT

COSTUME PLOT/WIGS

Git on Board

MISS PAT:
  two-piece pink and white mini skirt stewardess uniform
  white sleeveless blouse with Peter Pan collar
  pink and white uniform hard brim hat, exaggerated in
    size
  pink ankle strap hi-heels
  white cotton gloves
  shoulder-length straight black wig with a flip and bangs

WOMAN SLAVE:
  brown gauze tunic, tattered/distressed
  long brown head shawl

MEN SLAVES:
  brown diaper wrap, tattered/distressed

Cookin' with Aunt Ethel

AUNT ETHEL:
  heavy cotton textured black-and-rust blouse
  grey net cotton knotted scarf
  five-tier black, brown, red, and tan cotton skirt
  green and black small-check apron
  orange and black African print (distressed) head scarf

Photo Session

GIRL:
  red silk cowl neck gown with train
  gold leather belt
  red leather hi-heels
  red jewel earrings and necklace
  short high-fashion wig

GUY:
  black Eisenhower tux jacket
  black tux pants
  white wing-tip shirt with red bow tie
  red plaid cummerbund
  black lace-up shoes
  three jeweled rings

Soldier with a Secret

JUNIE:
  two-piece khaki green Army uniform, distressed
    and painted to blend with the onyx plinth
  large knapsack with double-crossed bullet belt
  green hard hat with net
  field boots

The Gospel According to Miss Roj

MISS ROJ:
  beige and gold sequined halter top
  orange, yellow, and gold striped satin sation pants
  elbow-length fingerless lace gloves with beads
  white leather go-go boots with hi-heels
  assorted rings
  cat-shaped sunglasses, jewel encrusted
  curly reddish-brown long wig

WAITER:
  aqua tee-shirt
  black jeans
  white tennis shoes

The Hairpiece

WOMAN:
  peach head towel
  peach body towel or peach satin robe
  peach fluffy slippers
  bald pate or stocking cap
  fake fingernails

JANINE:
  large oversized black Afro wig, á la Angela Davis,
    with bald pate/stocking cap underneath

LAWANDA:
  mid-back length straight, medium brown wig with
    bald pate/stocking cap underneath

The Last Mama-on-the-Couch Play

NARRATOR:
  black double-breasted tux jacket
  black tux pants
  white shirt
  black bow tie
  black leather slip-on shoes

MAMA:
  yellow faded floral cotton house dress, trim/collar
    made with doilies (*Note*: Dress matches the
    couch and drapes—see Property List.)
  beige cotton stockings, rolled to just below the
    knees
  black lace-up shoes
  short salt-and-pepper wig
  wire-rim glasses

WALTER-LEE-BEAU-WILLIE:
  mustard-colored cotton jacket, circa 1950s
  tan cotton work shirt
  dark khaki work pants
  brown gum-sole work boots

LADY IN PLAID:
  muslin cotton hand-painted plaid wrap dress with
    short sleeves and full skirt
  matching head scarf

MEDEA:
  60s pink and green abstract sleeveless blouse
  blue jeans, rolled cuffs
  three-inch leather belt
  poly/chiffon window sheer worn as a sash
  black and white saddle shoes
  white bobby socks
  short avant-garde wig, with a few thin long braids,
    black

Symbiosis

MAN:
  two-piece grey striped suit

white shirt
yellow silk paisley tie and pocket square
KID:
    denim sleeveless jacket covered with 60s patches
    "Jimi Hendrix" tee-shirt
    blue jeans
    black hi-top sneakers
    red "Apple Jack" cap

Lala's Opening
LALA:
    silk and gold lamé corseted "show girl" outfit,
        20s/30s style
    bronze and feather headress
    gold lamé whimsy cape with feathers
    gold glitter hi-heel dance shoes
    mid-back length curly black wig

ADMONIA:
    black and white 30s style maid uniform
    front ruffle mob cap
    black lace-up shoes*
    short salt-and-pepper wig*

FLO'RANCE:
    red silk smoking jacket
    white dress shirt (front only)
    black tux pants
    Caucasian realistic mask (full head) with blonde
        hair
    chest pad (see Property List)
    wine-colored silk cravat

LITTLE GIRL:
    pink chiffon party dress
    white tights
    white Mary Janes

_____

*ADMONIA wears the same wig and shoes MAMA wears in *The Last
Mama-on-the-Couch Play.*

Permutations

NORMAL JEAN:
light blue, full-skirt shirtwaist dress with a Peter
Pan collar
bobby socks
brown Abner boots

The Party

TOPSY WASHINGTON:
fuschia-colored satin top with black and pink
fringe
black spandex pants
blue glitter socks
black patent-leather hi-heel shoes
shoulder-length stylish-kinky black wig
a multitude of colorful jewelery—necklaces, arm
and ankle braclets, earrings, etc.

PROPERTY LIST/SET PIECES

Pre-set
3 stanchions with swag cables. The center stanchion has attached to it a framed sign which reads, "Next Exhibit at 8 PM".

Git on Board
overhead compartment
2 "Fasten Your Shackles" signs that light up
curtain—leading to offstage cockpit
shackles
basketball
assorted luggage
(3) I.D. luggage tags for slaves

Cookin' with Aunt Ethel
large, black cauldron, 2 feet in diameter, 3 feet in height, with dry ice to produce smoke effect.
stirring stick
2 Negroes (small black dolls)

Soldier with a Secret
onyx plinth enscribed with the words "Soldier with a Secret"

The Gospel According to Miss Roj
bar stool
round bar tray
6 drink glasses with ice and stirrers, half filled with liquor
neon sign: "The Bottomless Pit"

The Hairpiece
vanity table with two cut-out holes
vanity stool
trash can
photo in a frame
assorted make-up
several pairs of earrings on cards
telephone

The Last Mama-on-the-Couch Play
black bound script
stool for NARRATOR
acting award
picture of Jesus (built into the set)
beat-up old couch*
window unit with drapes*
2 life-sized black dolls (Cabbage Patch)
oversized Bible
2 Baptist church fans
four throw pillows
a black door mat

Symbiosis
dumpster
Saks Fifth Avenue bag, containing:
    a pair of Converse all-stars
    afro comb
    dashiki
    autographed pictures of Stokley Carmichael, Jomo
        Kenyatta, and Donna Summer
    Murray's pomade
    AfroSheen
    curl relaxer
    Soul on Ice
Albums:
    Jimi Hendrix's *Purple Haze*
    Sly Stone's *There's a Riot Goin' On*
    The Jackson Five's *I Want You Back*
    Stevie Wonder's *Fingertips Part 2*
    The Temptations' Greatest Hits
Buttons:
    Free Angela
    Free Bobby

---

*Please note: The couch and drapes should be of the same
material as the dress MAMA wears in this exhibit. See Costume
Plot.

Free Huey, Duey and Louie
U.S. out of Vietnam
U.S. out of Cambodia
U.S. out of Harlem, Detroit and Newark

Lala's Opening

Wireless mike
silver tray
letter opener
3 telegrams, folded and taped
sash cord for bonding FLO'RANCE
gag for FLO'RANCE
chair on casters
chest pad for the stabbing of FLO'RANCE—canvas
bodice, with 2½-inch foam attached to cowhide over
a metal breatplate

Permutations

large white egg, 36 inches long

DEATH in the POT

by Manuel Van Loggem

Poisonous mushrooms, red herrings, marital infidelities, and a mysterious Merchant of Death are elements in this English style **thriller** with a fascinating, intricate plot. Four males, two females; single interior set.

A riveting play, rich in texture and rife with allusion, which provides a chill-
ing vision of civilization about to go belly up. Originally produced at the
Los Angeles Theater Center in the summer of 1983. Seven males, three
females, though one more of each can be used. Single interior set plus an
exterior playing area.

BATTERY

BY DANIEL THERRIAULT

Electricity is the central metaphor and expressive image in this unusual love story which takes place in an electrical repair and systems design shop located in Chicago. Therriault has an exceptional ear for American speech patterns, and has been **compared to Sam Shepard and David Mamet for his superb use of language.** First produced in New York at St. Clement's Theater in the Spring of 1981. Two males, one female; single interior set.

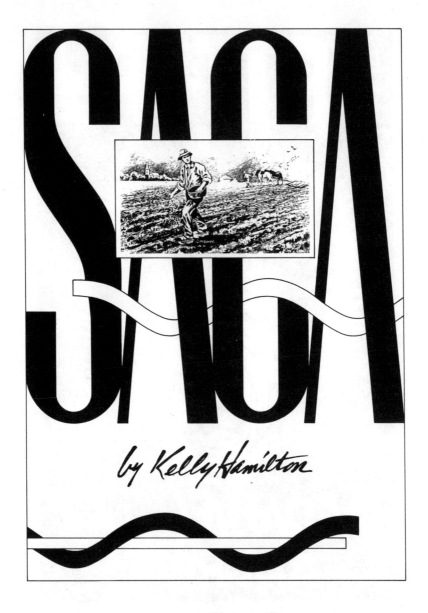

SAGA

by Kelly Hamilton

This wonderful **musical** is a history of America's pioneers as they push their way across the country. A minimum of eight males and eight females are necessary, and the show can be expanded to use many more actors. Settings can be fluid and simple or elaborate.

This delightful small scale **musical** is about the life of **Gilbert and Sullivan**. It is interspersed with some of the best known songs from the Savoy operas, including THE PIRATES OF PENZANCE, HMS PINAFORE and THE MIKADO. This show had a very successful run on the West End of London in 1975, and subsequently at the **Actors Theater of Louisville**. Five males, three females, though more actors may be used as "stage-hands" and chorus members.